Writing To Unlock Your You-est YOU™

GET A PHD IN YOU

Companion

Journal

JULIE REISLER

ISBN: 978-0-692-95297-9
Layout and Design by Christy Jenkins
Photo by anielle Visco, Luv Lens

Published by:
Empowered Living, LLC Books
1519 York Road
Lutherville, MD 21093

Dear Friend,
It's time to wakeup, arise,
and greet your highest self
in the mirror. Remember you are
guided, cherished, and loved, always.

Here's to Your You-est YOU!

~Julie Reisler

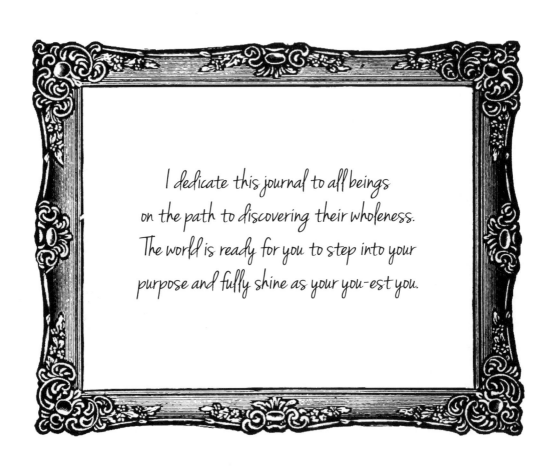

I dedicate this journal to all beings
on the path to discovering their wholeness.
The world is ready for you to step into your
purpose and fully shine as your you-est you.

Introduction

When you journal, you give yourself the greatest gift of all – time to connect more deeply to your highest self. This tool allows you to intentionally align with your most wise self, so that you are able to hear your inner voice more clearly. Journaling may help you feel closer to your creator, and to recognize that all you need already flows through you. The only requirement for you is to offer space to allow this opening for insights and answers to appear. I encourage you to pause, each day, to honor the moment and take stock of your thoughts, beliefs, dreams, and desires, as well as, your wobbles, woes, and worries.

Envision this...by pausing to write down what's cooking in your mind, you have the opportunity to add new ingredients, change the recipe, and feel gratitude for what you have already cooked up. It is within this expanse that you create what your next life buffet will be.

For me, each time I sit down to journal I experience what feels like magical alchemy. As I write down my inner thoughts, feelings, and goals, I awake to greater possibilities and ever-flowing connection to the Divine. I wish that for you, and it may be easier than you believe.

Free-flow, or what some call automatic writing, helps you to connect the dots of your life. Think of it as allowing yourself to come up for much needed fresh air that offers you the breathing room to check-in with yourself. Even taking a ten-minute break from your fast-paced life to assess where you are can help you to more consciously chart where you want to focus your precious energy. What we focus our attention on, expands.

Journaling can also help you develop your natural curiosity, which unfortunately, can shut down in a world where we feel the need to always be "right" and "safe," rather than open to new perspectives and possibilities. By remaining curious and open to new insights, you invite a higher wisdom into your life than your usual daily brain dishes up. So take a break, grab a cup of tea, and make space for your inner desires and dreams to appear.

I offer you this journal and the reminder to make space for yourself to help you awake to your true inner goodness. YOU are a miraculous Goddess meant to embody your divinity. Writing is a fabulous way to connect to a fuller experience of who YOU truly are. You are not simply the roles and tasks that you perform. You are so much more than that and journaling will help you to see that for yourself more clearly.

Remember that journal writing is a process. As I mentioned in Get a PhD in YOU, you will probably need to tell self-judgment and self-doubt to have a playdate elsewhere. It is normal to feel these "protectors" emerge as you start a new process. They can be an indication that old beliefs and behavior patterns need to be seen and released. A technique that I use when judgment arises is to imagine putting a large heart around emotions like doubt, fear, and worry. Instead of fighting against them, I give them room to just be as I flood them with love and compassion. Simply holding space for all feelings to co-exist, while putting the primary focus on our connection to our divine creator, can help resolve them with minimal effort.

By engaging your daily journal writing with optimism, you will meet new thoughts and ideas rooted in your innate desires and dreams that will serve your highest good. Remember, what you focus on grows. My hope for you is that YOU wake up to your fullest potential! No more pushing the snooze button on life—it's time for each of us to see everything we are being offered each day—the blessings, love, health, joy, and full self-expression that is our birthright.

I'd love to hear how this journal is helping you along your journey! Are you experiencing a whole new landscape and world of possibilities? Please stay in touch and share what's opening up for you. You can always find me for support and love at JulieReisler.com

Enjoy awakening to your journey!

With love & light,
Julie

P.S. Get your free love gift made just for YOU at juliereisler.com/journal.

Reflections on what needs to be released

PROMPT:

Can you recall a time you let something or someone go? How did that create a positive change in your life? What needs to release now?

I am not afraid of storms
for I am learning how to sail my ship.

~ Louisa May Alcott

You will never know what's possible
if you stay right where you are.
~ Julie Reisler

Knowing what must be done does away with fear.

~ Rosa Parks

Failure is impossible.

~ Susan B. Anthony

If it wasn't possible, your dream wouldn't exist. The thing that gets in the way of this possibility is your belief that it's not possible.

- Julie Reisler

Life shrinks or expands in proportion to one's courage.

~ Anais Nin

The most common way people give up their power
is by thinking they don't have any.

~ Alice Walker

Reflections on new self-awareness

PROMPT:

What have you been learning about yourself? How has your self-awareness added value to your life? What do you appreciate most about you?

Love yourself first, and everything else falls into line.

~ Lucille Ball

As you journal about your dreams, desires and goals, I invite you to pause and remember that all you wish for comes from the greatest creator of all — love.

- Julie Reisler

If you think taking care of yourself is selfish, change your mind.
If you don't, you're simply ducking your responsibilities.

~ Ann Richards

Everyone has inside of her a piece of good news. The good news is that you don't know how great you can be, how much you can love, what you can accomplish, and what your potential is.

~ Anne Frank

Journaling enables you to see through the cobwebs of your mind into the hidden words of your heart

~ Julie Reisler

Stop wearing your wishbone where your backbone ought to be.

~ Elizabeth Gilbert

The future belongs to those who believe in the beauty of their dreams.

~ Eleanor Roosevelt

Reflections on your dreams & purpose

PROMPT:
What dreams have come true
for you? What did that feel like?
When in your life have you felt
most purposeful or powerful?
Why?

All adventures, especially into new territory, are scary.

~ Sally Ride

Pure love is a beautiful high-frequency energy. Honor that you are unconditionally loved as a sacred being and remember that YOU are here to love yourself and others.

~ Julie Reisler

We do not need magic to change the world, we carry all the power we need inside ourselves already: we have the power to imagine better.

~ J.K. Rowling

Life is either a daring adventure or nothing.

~ Helen Keller

You will never know what's
possible if you stay right
where you are.

~ Julie Reisler

Just don't give up trying to do what you really want to do.
Where there is love and inspiration, I don't think you can go wrong.

~ Ella Fitzgerald

Life is not about finding yourself. Life is about creating yourself.

~ Lolly Daskal

PROMPT:
How do you want to fully express yourself in the world? What actions will make a difference and enhance your life? List things, people, and experiences you have manifested thus far.

The starting point of all achievement is desire.

~ Napolean Hill

When you allow yourself to play
and have more fun, the return on
investment in your life is priceless.

– Julie Reisler

The most effective way to do it, is to do it

~ Amelia Earhart

You are the one that possesses the keys to your being.
You carry the passport to your own happiness.

~ Diane von Furstenberg

I continuously launder my mind, words and thoughts, so that I'm left with sweet smelling beliefs serving my highest good and that of the world.

- Julie Reisler

When the whole world is silent,
even one voice becomes powerful.

~ Malala Yousafzai

If you don't risk anything, you risk even more.

~ Erica Jong

Reflections on appreciation

PROMPT:

What we focus on expands.
What can you focus on right now
that is going well in your life?
Where can you add more appreciation
to your day-to-day moments and
mundane tasks? What are 20
things you are appreciative of
right now?

Make the most of yourself by fanning the tiny, inner sparks
of possibility into flames of achievement.

~ Golda Meir

The single most important ingredient often
missing from the main dish of life is appreciation.
When you combine appreciation with focusing
on the moment, you're left to savor the most
delicious sensory meal imaginable.

- Julie Reisler

I didn't get there by wishing for it or hoping for it, but by working for it

~ Estee Lauder

The purpose of our lives is to be happy.

~ Dalai Lama

Journaling enables you to see the cobwebs of your mind and the hidden words in your heart wanting expression. There is magic in finding the keys to your best self and to being greeted by empowerment, faith, excitement and miracles.

– Julie Reisler

You grow up the day you have your first real laugh at yourself.

~ Ethel Barrymore

Life shrinks or expands in proportion with one's courage.

~ Anais Nin

Reflections about finding unconditional love

PROMPT:

How do you define
unconditional love?
What are ways you can begin
showing unconditional love
to yourself?
How can you be more loving
to all beings?

Only do what your heart tells you.

~ Princess Diana

Since your mind can only truly focus on one thing at a time, you might as well choose what's most incredible in your life right now.

~ Julie Reisler

I know for sure that what we dwell on is what we become.

~ Oprah Winfrey

Do you really want to look back on your life and see
how wonderful it could have been had you not been afraid to live in?

~ Caroline Myss

The presence of now + appreciation
for all that's going well = unleashed joy,
inner-peace and happiness.

~ Julie Reisler

It's not your job to like me, it's mine.

~ Byron Katie

Without leaps of imagination, or dreaming, we lose the excitement of possibilities. Dreaming, after all, is a form of planning.

~ Gloria Steinem

Unlocking the You-est YOU

Journaling is a daily practice that reaps rewards time and time again. I have found that journaling for as little as five minutes a day creates positive ripple effects in all areas of my life. The best part is affirming my intention to be my most authentic self each day.

I invite and encourage you to commit to this practice, whether it is using the writing prompts I've given you or your own process. There is no wrong way to journal. There is only the invitation to connect to the true YOU.

I wish for you a joyful journey of becoming more and more of who you truly are. May you understand more about why you chose to be on this planet at this time. May your sacred words, thoughts and insights help you to believe that you are a worthy, divine and blessed human being living your soul's purpose.

May you realize and actualize your truest, You-est YOU.

With love,
Julie

65040314R00084

Made in the USA
San Bernardino, CA
27 December 2017